Table of Contents

Foreword	9
OKR Story	12
MBOs	12
SMART	14
KPIs	14
The Evolution of OKRs	15
The Anatomy of OKRs	16
How OKR Works and Why It Became a Global Management Performance Phenomenon	17
Objectives	19
Key Results (KRs)	21
Initiatives	23
OKR Benefits	24
Focus	24
Establishes Indicators for Measuring Progress	24
Creates Organizational Discipline by Alignment	25
Builds Community and Fulfilling Experience	25
The 4 Principles of OKRs	25
1- Focus and Commit to Priorities	26
2. Align and Connect for Teamwork	28
3. Track for Accountability	30
4. Stretch Goals. Rethinking What's Possible	32
How Google Perfected OKRs	34
The Google Chrome Story	35

The Gmail Story	36
The Youtube Story	37

The Top Ideation Tools to Create OKRs — 39
- 1. Brainwriting vs. Brainstorming — 40
- Brainwriting Steps — 40
  - The Top Softwares for Brainwriting — 41
- 2. Design Thinking — 42
  - The 5 Stages of Design Thinking — 43
    - 1. Empathize — 43
    - 2. Define (The Problem) — 44
    - 3. Ideate — 44
    - 4. Prototype — 45
    - 5. Test — 45

How to Implement Design Thinking into Your Organization — 46
- 1. Focus on the Problem. — 46
- 2. Encourage Design Thinking on Your Team. — 47
- 3. Encourage Rapid Failure — 47
- 4. Mind Mapping — 48

How Companies 10x Their Performance via OKRs — 49
- Defining the Top Objectives — 49

The Hierarchy of OKRs — 51

Setting Company OKRs — 51

Setting Team and Individual OKRs — 52

Key Characteristics of Objectives — 52

Key Characteristics of Key Results — 54

Key Characteristics of Initiatives	54
OKR CHECKLIST	**55**
General	55
Objectives	55
Key Results	56
Initiatives	56
Timeline	56
How Grading Works	**57**
How to Create a Sustainable OKR Environment	**58**
How to Become an OKR Expert	**58**
Individual OKR Examples	60
Business	60
Family	61
Personal	61
How to Master OKR as a Company	**62**
Consistency	62
Ambitious	63
Feedback Loop	63
Open Culture	63
Free Space	64
How to Implement CFR for Continuous Performance Management	**64**
Conversations	65
Feedback	66
Recognition	67
The Best Free and Paid OKR Tools / Softwares	**69**

Google Docs / Google Sheets	69
Koan	70
Coda	70
Weekdone	70
Plai	71
OKRs vs Other Top Performance Systems	**71**
OKRs vs KPIs	72
KPI Examples	72
OKRs vs SMART	73
OKRs vs Balanced Scorecard	74
Top Reads	**75**
Top OKR Sources	75
OKR and Performance Related Top Books	75
Author's Books	76
Helium Network: The Best Crypto Mining Choice : Earn up to $10,000 per month passively anywhere in the world while building the People's Network of IoT and 5G:	**76**
The Best Video Learning Sources for OKR	**77**
References	**78**
About the Author	**79**

Foreword

Human capacity is limitless. What limits our capacity is how we create and manage our goals, how we execute to achieve them and how we manage our time. If we learn how to set truly challenging, yet achievable goals, executing a plan around them, and building the discipline to check on them regularly, **we can 10x our performance, and this is what this book is about.**

According to John Doerr who is one of the key personalities for making OKRs a global phenomenon: "Ideas are easy, execution is everything."

When I turn my eyes onto how huge companies, such as Google, works, it always amazes me how they are able to innovate consistently for many years when I know that most people have a hard time managing their own lives for continuous growth.

How come a company with over 70,000 employees work and achieve goals as one living organism while keeping innovative as if they are a small startup? The answer is about defining What and How clearly for each individual bearing in mind the end goal or vision of the company created by the executive team and taking their own role to build the system for the company to achieve that goal.

I have long been saying that if Google does it, I use it. Google's culture of simplistic sophistication is clear as you use all their services starting from the search engine to its Google Drive, Gmail and many more services.

And behind all those giant businesses within the company, lies the OKR system's incredibly effective performance framework that is as simple and effective as the Google search home page itself, which hardly changed since 1998.

OKR stands for Objectives and Key Results. Basically, for a company, the first objectives or top priorities are set by the executive team, which corresponds to the "What" of the company , and KRs, Key Results, work as "How" of the company.

Today, hundreds of top companies from all fields adopted OKRs as their performance tool to achieve their goals as an organization. Some examples include Amazon, Spotify, Linkedin, Box, Salesforce, Netflix, Twitter, Vice Media, Uber, and many more.

The OKR performance framework can be used for any size company and it can also be a very effective tool for individual use. OKR makes the goal-setting and metrics to achieve those goals simply to create, check and implement by creating the individual and team discipline around the top priorities.

According to Larry Page, the co-founder and former CEO of Google, "OKRs have helped us to 10x growth, many times over. They've helped make our crazily bold mission of organizing the world's information perhaps even achievable. They've kept me and the rest of the company on time and on track when it mattered the most.

This book is to gain you an understanding of how OKR works concisely so that you can also use it to boost your company's and your own performance by 10x as many top companies and individuals have done.

Let's start with How the OKR phenomenon started and became the backbone of one of the most innovative companies in the world, Google.

OKR Story

OKRs were first introduced by Andrew Grove, "Father of OKRs", to Intel during his tenure there. He then wrote a book, High Output Management, in 1983.

MBOs

The inspiration and experience of OKRs were initially started by Peter Drucker who introduced Management by Objectives (MBOs) in 1954, in which management and employees agree upon objectives and what they need to do to achieve them.

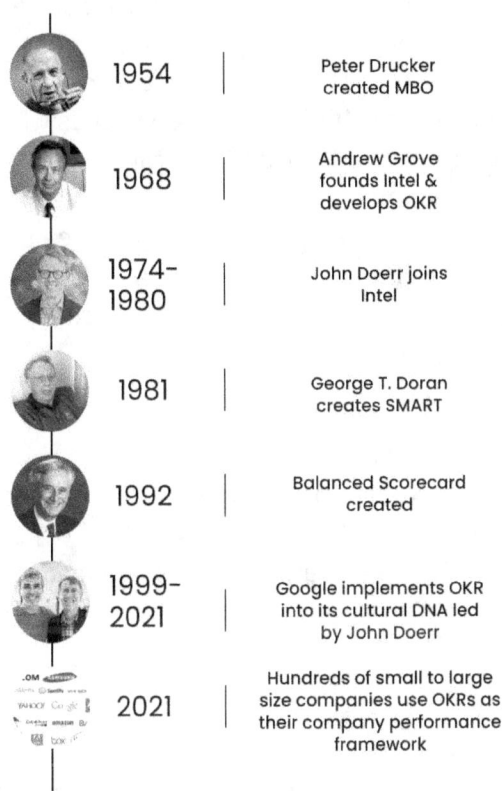

OKR Timeline

Even though MBOs are similar to OKRs in the sense that they determine objectives, there are major differences between them.
- MBOs can be qualitative or quantitative while OKRs are always quantitative, OKRs have a data-driven approach.

- An MBO is basically a set of detailed objectives while an OKR details the objective and designs the roadmap of how the team will reach that objective.
- An MBO aims for 100% objective success while an OKR aims for a 60-80% success rate.

There are two other management performance tools, namely, S.M.A.R.T. and KPIs, that became extremely popular in the early 80s, which also influenced the OKRs as we know them today.

SMART

S.M.A.R.T was created by George T. Doran, stands for Specific, Measurable, Achievable, Results, Focused, and Time-bound. OKR was partially influenced by SMART, particularly results-focused and time-bound elements of SMART.

KPIs

KPIs, which stands for Key Performance Indicators, introduced metric-validated performance evaluation for companies. Even though KPIs may look similar to OKRs at first sight, there are major differences. KPIs are good if you're working on a project that has already been done before looking for a 100% success rate and OKRs are normally the choice of managerial performance framework if you want to achieve new and ambitious goals with possibly a 70% success rate.

The Evolution of OKRs

As OKR evolved from MBO, KPI, and SMART, John Doerr, who worked as a sales manager in Intel under Andy Grove, became the global ambassador of OKRs thanks to his introduction of the management and growth concept to Google in 1999.

The Anatomy of OKRs

According to John Doerr, OKRs should work as follows: " The key result has to be measurable, but at the end, you can look and without any arguments: Did I do that or did I not do it? Yes or No? Simple. No judgments in it."

Objective
What is my top priority?

Objectives are statements that set direction and inspire.

Key Results
How I know how far I'm getting?

Key Results measure your progress toward an objective.

Initiatives
What will I do to get there?

Initiatives are the actions taken to make progress on Key Results.

The 3 Steps of OKRs

Then, hundreds of small to large companies embraced OKRs into their cultures such as Linkedin, GoPro, Spotify, Edmunds, Flipboard, and many more.

As Google has grown from 40 to over 70,000 people, the OKR innovation management system has been the backbone for every employee's daily work process as well as creating the necessary discipline to achieve the ultimate objective of making the world of information open to everyone in the world possible while aligning the company with the same goal for over 20 years.

How OKR Works and Why It Became a Global Management Performance Phenomenon

We live in a fast-paced world with hundreds of distractions a day even in our individual lives. Without clearly defined goals and a timely plan to achieve them, it's easy to lose our direction and the energy for achievement.

Also, if we're not working on something repetitive such as making coffee or commuting for our work and rather if we want to achieve new challenging and long-term goals such as building a company, learning a new skill, or slow-traveling the world as a nomad, then, we need to set our priorities and how we will achieve them while defining a timeline for each goal.

This is where OKR comes in, which builds a well-structured system around setting challenging goals and measurable key results to achieve those goals.

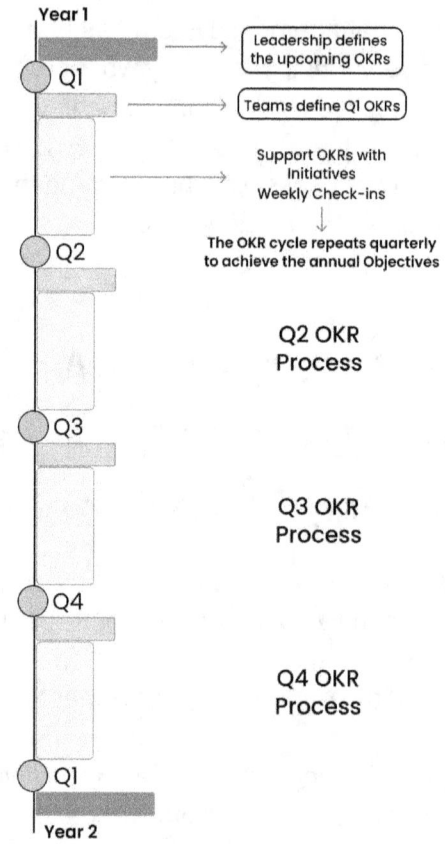

How OKRs Work Annually within a Company

Objectives

In order for any company or individual to succeed, the top priorities need to be defined. In the context of companies, the ultimate objective, which is ideally the combination of vision and mission, is set by the top executive team.

Let's test this approach with Amazon, the biggest retailer in the world.

Amazon Vision. "Our vision is to be earth's most customer-centric company; to build a place where people can come to find and discover anything they might want to buy online."

Amazon Mission Statement. "We strive to offer our customers the lowest possible prices, the best available selection, and the utmost convenience."

Then, this life-long company objective creates side objectives with each of them having their 3-5 key results. Objectives are well-thought-out and concise.

From the above Amazon vision and mission statement, we can infer that Amazon's ultimate objective would have the following at its center: *Customer-centric, faster and cheaper products , and the best available selection.*

Amazon's ultimate objective: "Build the most customer-centric store that sells everything."

Objectives answer the question "What?" and define the top priorities.

Below are the main principles of how objectives work:
- Objectives are single sentences and concise goals that set the priorities.
- Apart from the ultimate objective, there are normally annual and quarterly objectives.
- Objectives set high and challenging goals.
- As objectives are created to build clarity over priorities, there cannot be more than 3-5 objectives annually for each part of the company.
- Objectives are immeasurable. They are meant to determine the direction of the company and where most energy will be spent within the given period of time.
- Objectives are inspirational and compelling goals that move the company or person from their comfort zone. However, they are still achievable with extraordinary performance.
- Objectives are open to the entire company. All company OKRs, including the one of the CEO, are open for the view of the whole company. This creates transparency and community for the entire company to align to.
- Objectives are time-bound. OKR is the growth management system for companies or individuals to create the priorities, how to achieve them, within the predetermined time frame.
- Objectives are actionable by the team independently. This is particularly important for larger companies since

interdependency may result in gridlocks among teams to achieve the goals.
- For organization-level OKRs, the senior leadership must personally commit to the process of becoming an example for the entire company.

Key Results (KRs)

KRs ask the question "How?" and they are the means to reach the objectives.

Let's work on a few Key Results in different fields.

An OKR for Engineering.
Objective: Reduce outsourcing by 30% in the next 6 months.
Key Result 1. Scale up the R&D department by 50% in Q2.
Key Result 2. Manufacture the product with 10% fewer parts in 6 months.
Key Result 3. Acquire 2 companies with maximum spending of $35M in the next 6 months.

An OKR for Fashion.
Objective: Launch a sportswear product line that sells $1M in a year.
Key Result 1. Create 5 design concepts in 1 month.
Key Result 2. Find the manufacturing partner in a month that is able to produce 10,000 shirts a day with a cost of $7 for each shirt.

Key Result 3. Build a fashion content creator partner network of 20 people for the US market.

An OKR for Sales
Objective: Reach 5M sales for the new product line in Q4.
Key Result 1. Open 3 physical stores in New York, San Francisco, and Los Angeles.
Key Result 2. Add all the new products into Amazon fashion and launch targeted ads with a $10k/mo budget.
Key Result 3. Work with 5 content creators to reach 10M engaged followers.

Below are the most important criteria of how KRs work:
- KRs must be quantified. Measuring the key results creates clarity regarding the success rate, which is key to performance evaluation. As Marissa Mayer, the 6th employee of Google says: "It's not a key result unless it has a number." This is how a KR performance is evaluated, there is no gray area, no room for doubt.
- The number of Key Results should be limited to 3 to 5. Just as for objectives, if there are over 5 KRs, then, the rate of achieving those results significantly decreases. Therefore, it is essential that the right KRs are set with achievable, but challenging numbers to reach.
- Key Results should be checked regularly. As each time period milestone is reached, the progress should be inspected by the individual and the team giving them the feedback necessary to update the status and what steps need to be taken to achieve the targeted performance.
- KRs are graded from 0 to 1. KRs need to be set so that it should almost be impossible to score 1. Generally

speaking, a score of 0.6 to 0.7 is regarded as successful where a score lower than 0.4 is regarded as a low point.

Initiatives

Initiatives are the actions taken by the company or individuals to reach the key results. Initiatives are what you will do to get there.

Objective. Become a UI/UX designer building modern designs for startups.
Key Result 1. Build a professional mobile app for a startup for free in 3 months.
The below 3 initiatives are to be implemented to achieve Key Result 1.
Initiative 1. Finish 3 online courses spending 3 hours a day in a month.
Initiative 2. Hire a senior designer and take a 20-hour class after finishing the 3 courses.
Initiative 3. Build a copycat of a mobile app in two months.

Timeline
OKRs are time-bound. A certain timeline needs to be set to achieve objectives and key results within the pre-defined timeframe. Mostly, companies have quarterly and annual timeframes, however, this period may be shorter for small startups and individuals.

OKR Benefits

OKR gains long-term benefits for the companies and individuals alike creating a 10x performance culture.

Focus

The OKR system gains focus on the individual and the company and this can only happen if the number of OKRs is 3 to 5 for a certain period of time, quarterly or annually. Basically, if you focus on everything, then, you focus on nothing.
Since all the OKRs are publicly open and inspected regularly for performance, the goals and progress stay aligned within the organization.

Establishes Indicators for Measuring Progress

As the individual and/or company gains focus with the 3-5 objectives prioritizing the goals, the key results quantify the evaluation of the performance, which gains clarity about reaching the objective.
By making regular inspections of the Key Results, you learn how far away you are from the goal, which creates invaluable feedback for where you stand, and what you should do.

Creates Organizational Discipline by Alignment

OKRs create the framework for the selection, execution, inspection, progress, and implementation of the top priorities whether it is designed for an individual or the largest companies such as Google or Spotify.
It brings complete alignment no matter the size of the company since all the company OKRs are open to everyone in the company, which gives the ability to regularly check and update so that all employees feel connected and responsible for achieving the top priorities.

Builds Community and Fulfilling Experience

When the individual or company knows its priorities and designs the process themselves, then the life and job satisfaction hits new highs while building the community and solidarity among partakers because they share the common goals and support each other to reach there.

The 4 Principles of OKRs

Building an effective OKR culture requires a continuous setting of certain disciplines to build the fundamentals of an organically accepted and applied innovation system.

1- Focus and Commit to Priorities

As Steve Jobs puts it, " Success and focus are about saying no." The OKRs build the structure to build the foundation of goal-setting in a simple yet sophisticated way, which allows the flexible growth of an individual's life and the largest companies such as Google with over 70,000 people for over 20+ years.

Firstly, the ultimate objective or the top priority needs to be set answering the question: "What?" for the individual or the company.

The top exec team needs to determine the top objective, stand firmly behind a few top-line OKRs, and model the disciplined path for the entire company creating an example of commitment, far-reaching goals, and openness.

As the top long-term objectives are created by the exec team and clearly understood throughout the organization, then, the departments, teams and individuals can create their own objectives and key results for the quarter, and year, which would be open for the entire company.

As Phil Knight, the founder of Nike, puts it: "Guide people about what to do and let them find out 'how' it will be done."

Also, Steve Jobs said "It doesn't make sense to hire smart people and tell them what to do. We hire smart people so they can tell us what to do."

Interestingly, today, two out of three companies fail to communicate the objectives clearly to the organization. In a survey of more than 10 thousand managers, the majority couldn't name the top priorities of their companies.

The management of the company needs to create the meaning behind the objectives answering the question "Why?" as well as "What?", which creates the motivation and company culture, a company that lives by common values with clarity.

As the objectives are well-framed and set, the key results to achieve those goals need to be defined. Ideally, the number of KRs is 3-5 making each of them clear, quantifiable, challenging, yet achievable. Key results need to make sure you become your best in achieving the goals.

There is nothing more powerful than putting a deadline to achieve a goal that would otherwise look not possible. As objectives and key results create laser focus around the top priorities, what needs to be set is the timeframe to achieve those goals.

In order for "focus" to be fully effective, the feedback cycle needs to be frequent and occur as soon as the activity is completed so that timely decisions can be made improving and fine-tuning the process creating a road map gradually designing to reach the ultimate goals.

One major flaw to prevent from happening would be focusing on a certain part of development while neglecting and possibly worsening another part. A good example could be creating a great product not thinking about the cost of logistics or the customer profile. The OKR thought process should be formed so that it doesn't adversely affect the other parts of the company.

OKRs requiring commitment don't mean that they are untouchable. Both the objectives and key results can be changed or terminated if they are seen as not serving the priorities of the company or the individual.

Another important point to bear in mind is that all key results need to serve the purpose of attaining the objective. If not, then, it's not an OKR.

2. Align and Connect for Teamwork

Especially when organizations scale, and work remotely, there needs to be a system that creates organic alignment among the departments, teams, and individuals.

As Google and many other small to large companies clearly indicate after many years, OKRs create simplicity in communicating the periodic goals and key results openly while inspecting the progress periodically.

Even though the alignment is an essential part of any teamwork, studies suggest that only 7% of employees fully understand their company's strategies and priorities, which results in working in the wrong direction, therefore, misalignment and the poor use of available sources.

The traditional management model embraces cascading, which means the strategies and actions move from the top to the bottom hierarchically, from the top exec team to the department managers, and so on without having open communication, which causes miscommunication and misalignment as it moves down the management ladder.

OKRs take the open perspective, which embraces the bottom-up approach that communicates the top priorities and objectives openly among all the departments. This creates a healthy environment of open development in which each member of the company takes an active role knowing the strategies and actions of all clearly.

Micromanagement should be avoided especially as the company scales and this is exactly what OKRs are designed for.

As the objectives or "What" is known, then, key results or "How" it's done are strategized and executed by the employees autonomously.

An ideal OKR leaves the creation of at least some of the objectives and key results to the employees, which creates the feeling of ownership and deeper awareness for what's needed to achieve the results.

When our "how" is defined by others, then, our bond with it won't be truly ours. As we free the minds of people working with us, we not only create a deeper relation, but also create the foundation of open innovation that all team members become truly engaged.

The best part of truly open communication is that if the team or individual makes outstanding progress, you immediately see it and if the team is far behind the target, then, it's again instantly visible for all to investigate and take the right measures so that all is aligned.

3. Track for Accountability

Apart from building the main framework for progress, OKRs also serve as a living organism making sure that they best serve the company goals.

Since all company OKRs are open internally, any OKR that's left behind can be investigated and improved. Contributors can also check at will how their work contributes to the company's success.

Grading is how the success of the Key Results is determined and it ranges from 0 to 1.

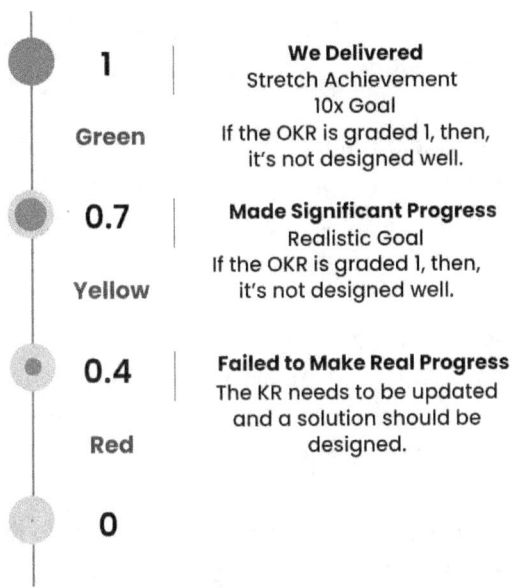

How OKR Grading Works with a scale from 0 to 1

In large companies, grading can be automated by advanced software taking into account objective criteria to quantify the implementation. However, it may also be done by the employee or team objectively.

Contributors are most engaged when they can actually see how their work contributes to the company's success.

Normally, a 0.6 - 0.7 mark is the goal for the KR. Goals need to be achievable, however, they also need to be challenging.

Grading is a means of feedback and it should not be seen as the success or failure of the employee or the team. If so, then, a risk-averse culture would become inevitable.

Also, OKRs should not be connected with compensation since doing so would again create a culture that would avoid risks while creating a company that gains its motivation from financial gains.

As the grading is made, the achievement can be celebrated and each completion of an OKR means that the results need to be evaluated for further improvement while considering the next steps.

Grading can be made individually and manually as well as using software, especially for larger companies. Whether done using pen and paper, free or paid software, all OKRs should be measurable so that it is objectively graded using any tool.

4.Stretch Goals. Rethinking What's Possible

Stretch goals are about making the seemingly impossible, possibly achievable.

They lead us to achieve dream goals. In Google's case, this is making the entire world of information open for the whole world, which would seemingly be impossible in 1999 as Larry Page, the Google co-founder thought what OKR made possible. Now, after using OKR for over 20 years, it's an achievable goal for the company.

An alternative way to what stretch goals actually mean is seeing them as the source of innovation. Innovation is about making the extraordinary and new useful product become a reality and this is exactly what OKR is created for.

"Stretch goals gain a deeper engagement and make people more productive and motivated."

Steve Jobs' and Elon Musks' "reality distortion field" may be ideal examples for stretch goals. Steve Jobs believed that every home in the world can have personal computers and Elon Musk believed in the sustainable features through electric vehicles. As they created these top goals for their companies and built the company culture around them, their goals and achievements took the shape of these extraordinary visions, which made the companies and then, people around the world believe in them.

Realizing stretch goals requires resourceful resilience and an unbeatable vision. It's about making it possible. Dreams for tomorrow become a reality and then, another chapter opens with even a broader perspective as more experience and resources are gained.

Google divides its goals into two segments, which are committed goals and aspirational or stretch goals.

Committed goals are basically everyday goals for most companies such as realizing the sales numbers or timely shipment of new products. These are to be achieved 100% within a set timeframe. On the other hand, stretch goals are considerably challenging goals that are unlikely to be achieved 100%. They become the goal that the department, team, or individuals ultimately aim to reach using all the sources and energy available.

How Google Perfected OKRs

Google owes much of its hypergrowth and making "all the information in the world available for everyone" achievable by the systemic innovation discipline and open alignment throughout the company for over 20 years.

Thanks to John Doerr's introduction of the OKR framework and the commitment of the founding team including the co-founders, Larry Page and Sergey Brin, Google's culture accomplished to have an innovative reflex of a startup while having over 70,000 Googlers.

Google is the best living proof that a company with just 40 people can innovate non-stop for over 20 years to become one of the biggest and most innovative companies in the world using the OKR system at its cultural core.

The Google Chrome Story

Google products have their own way, starting from Google search. The user experience is simple and intuitive and yet, sophisticated and fast.

This culture originates from the founders, Larry Page and Sergey Brin. By 2006, Google was already rethinking the browser experience as a computing platform, almost like an operating system that could write applications on the web itself.

In 2008, Larry and Sergey wrote an OKR that created the vision behind the Chrome browser and then, platform: "We should make the web as fast as flipping through a magazine."

Starting from point zero, the stretch goal for the Chrome browser was to have a stretch goal of having 20 million weekly active users by the end of the first year, 2008.

One of the major key results of the Google Chrome objective was to create a never-seen blazing-fast Javascript experience. The goal was to create a 10x faster browser than Mozilla Firefox. Fortunately, Google was able to hire a Danish software genius, Lars Bak and he promised a 10x faster browser than Firefox. Within two years, it was more than 20 times faster.

This clearly proves that a seemingly impossible goal can be achieved once the team has 100% focus. OKRs don't need to be completed within a year. Google Chrome aimed for 20 million weekly active users and failed. Google then aimed for 50 million weekly active users for 2009 and reached 38 million and finally, in 2010, Google created almost warp speed compared to other browsers and changed the speed of the internet by 10x, many times over what was conceived as not possible, thanks to OKRs.

The Gmail Story

In the early 2000s, the main issue with a web-based email system was the lack of storage. All email providers including Yahoo and Hotmail used to provide 2 to 4 MB of storage space, which was unacceptable. As soon as you receive new emails, you would need to free some space deleting files and emails from before.

Google came up with an ambitious goal of providing 1 GB of space for free, which would be up to 500 times more than the competition, which changed email and digital communication forever.

This is again a clear instance of How Google culture is shaped by audacious goals that are designed to rethink the problem and create 10x solutions.

To rethink what's possible, they needed to change their perspective, find new partners, move resources and create an uncomfortably exciting environment to make the team believe and reach the goals as close as possible within the given timeframe.

Google is one of the most global mindset companies of the world working on having 1 billion+ users for any product they launch and Googlers who are already top achievers feel they are working on products, which are bigger than themselves, possibly affecting how the world works.

Therefore, by setting extraordinarily ambitious goals while measuring the success using the KRs, the biggest technology team of over 70,000 people is able to do seemingly impossible challenges and create global products that are used daily.

The Youtube Story

Back in 2006, by the time Google videos started to compete with Youtube, which was founded in 2005, Youtube already claimed a significant market share because of its fast uploading technology.

Therefore, Susan Wojcicki, the 16th employee of Google convinced the Google leadership that the Youtube price tag of $1.65 billion was worth it to become the leading video platform of the world.

In the early days, the metrics to develop the platform to the next level were unclear. That resulted in ambiguity and a lack of clear goals.

Then, it was clarified that the most important priority for Youtube was "watch time". More openly, the goal was to increase the number of viewers as well as the amount of time each viewer spends watching videos daily.

More watch time meant more ad revenue, more and revenue meant more motivation for content creators, which corresponds to more organic growth of the platform. This was done responsibly by not promoting clickbait or tabloid videos and finding ways to guide for rich content.

As the main growth metric was defined, it was time to create the main OKR of the company. After a long debate, the one sentence and the easy-to-understand audacious goal was determined as: reaching 1 billion hour weekly watch time in 4 years. This was clearly a stretch goal and more specifically, it was 10x more than the watch time at the time.

The goal would possibly sound impossible to most of people, but Google changed its framing and instead of reaching a 10x scale, they framed it as reaching 20% of the world's total TV watch time.

Also, the 4-year OKR was broken down into a set of annual objectives and incremental key results, which created the frequent inspection, feedback cycle needed to make updates and adjustments along the way.

By October 2016, the goal of a 1 billion hours weekly watch time bar was surpassed. For Youtube, it became a religion for 4 years embraced by every Youtube overcoming many challenges such as bandwidth or gaining new users while keeping the quality of the content.

As the platform continues to grow, new metrics are found with the rising needs, which create new OKRs.

The Top Ideation Tools to Create OKRs

Ideation refers to the process of how the idea will be implemented. Ideation works preferably for a business setting. It can be expressed in graphical, written, or verbal terms.

To start the ideation process, the problem needs to be clearly defined. The questions to ask could be about the underlying factors, industry trends, business environment, customer needs, budget constraints, etc.

There are a number of great tools to ideate that companies use to create brilliant top ideas that then become company objectives.

I want to share with you my top ideation tools that are most effective, creative, and practical.

1. Brainwriting vs. Brainstorming

Almost everyone knows brainstorming. We actually do it almost every day when we want to make decisions or create solutions, especially when a group of people is involved.

Brainstorming is a method of generating ideas by asking the ideas orally to a group of people.

- Ideally, the process takes 15-45 minutes.
- The number of people is 5 to 7.
- All ideas are collected from a group of people and written down.

Brainwriting on the other hand is asking each member of the group to write down their ideas about a particular problem.

Brainwriting Steps

- The moderator introduces the topic to 6 people sitting around the table.
- Each participant writes 3 ideas in 5 minutes.
- Then, each of them passes their sheet to the one on the right.
- This continues until everyone in the group enters 3 ideas underneath each person's ideas following the idea pattern.

- In the end, in only 30 minutes, each person writes 18 ideas, which results in 18 x 6 = 108 ideas overall.

Brainwriting has a number of advantages over brainstorming.
- **No interruption.** Since brainstorming is done orally, it's not designed for introverts and the louder voice can win the room whereas brainwriting gives everyone the same chance to bring up their insights and creativity.
- **Form of communication.** Brainwriting is a great way to keep all ideas under record. Also, it urges more creativity than brainstorming since people are given the time to add their ideas to other people's ideas, which feeds the creativity.
- **More ideas.** With brainwriting in only a matter of 30 minutes, the group has 108 ideas, which can then become objectives for innovating the OKR.

The Top Softwares for Brainwriting

There are a number of brainwriting software that can significantly ease the process. We have two clear winners that you can use the top Brainwriting tool.
- **Tecmark.** The software is practical and effective by timing the ideation process while giving private time for participants. You can see more here.
- **Stormz.** This app has great collaboration and voting tools, which facilitates the ideation process. This tool has many features, therefore, you may need to go over the tutorials. You can see more here.

2. Design Thinking

Design thinking is also named human-centered design. The user experience is in the center to create new products, services, and processes and anyone can become a design thinker as long as they understand the problem to solve and follow the guideline of design thinking.

As IDEO founder David Kelley suggests, "creative confidence is the belief that everyone is creative, and that creativity isn't the ability to draw or compose or sculpt, but a way of understanding the world."

The Interaction where design thinking lives according to designthinking.ideo.com

Companies using Design Thinking include Google, Airbnb, Starbucks, Apple, Toyota, Microsoft, Nike, Burberry, Bank of America, and many more.

The 5 Stages of Design Thinking

The 5 stages of Design Thinking proposed by Hasso-Plattner Institute of Design at Stanford (d.school), the leading school teaching design thinking, is as follows:

Empathize, Define (the problem), Ideate, Prototype, and Test.

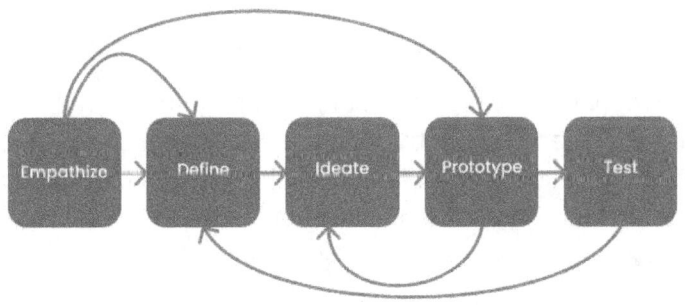

Design Thinking is a 5-Stage Process

1. Empathize

A product or service can seem to be fine for you, however, the general user experience could be totally different.

The way to initiate Design Thinking is to start understanding the user to create a human-centered design.

Empathy allows design thinkers to set their own assumptions aside in order to gain a deeper understanding of the world around them.

In order to achieve this understanding, active curiosity about all aspects of the problem is key. The idea is to collect information about the users' needs, their requests, and the problems faced to develop a particular product.

2. Define (The Problem)

With all the information gathered, the core problem can be defined having a human-centered design mindset.

The "define" process will create the bridge between Empathize and Ideate by giving design thinkers the opportunity to establish features, elements, and problems that ultimately generate the foundation for the next stage, Ideate.

3. Ideate

At this stage, design thinkers generate ideas having gained a deep understanding of the core problem following the Empathize stage, which lets them understand the user experience, and the Define stage, which lets them create the human-centered problem statement.

There are a number of techniques that can be used such as Brainstorming, Brainwriting, Delphi Technique, Worst Possible Idea, or Mind Mapping.

Among these techniques, if you have a group of people, then, the best method could be brainwriting to create a great number of ideas that matter for the user in a short period of time. You may use the brainwriting section for guidance to apply that method.

If you are an individual, then, you may want to use Mind Mapping since that is graphical as well as textual matching the context of a design thinker.

4. Prototype

The goal of this stage is to build fast and inexpensive prototypes to receive feedback from the users. Prototypes are built for each idea and shared with a small number of people outside the design team.

By the end of this stage, the possible solutions are investigated and the decision is made if they will be accepted, re-examined, improved, or rejected.

This way, a clear view is gained with regards to how real users experience the product or service.

5. Test

Following the prototype stage, it's time to test the final product as the best ideas are implemented.

The goal of this stage is to make a few improvements and refinements as needed.

Design Thinking, human-centered design, is the way that any company can adopt into its culture to create great products/services while using OKRs as their performance framework.

How to Implement Design Thinking into Your Organization

The most fundamental piece of design thinking is understanding the needs and feedback of the end-users so that you don't work on the wrong content from the start.

1. Focus on the Problem.

The key to finding the core problem is listening to your users and keeping a curious and open mind while learning more about possible changes you can make.

You need to stay unbiased about the problem and the solution and you might discover other findings that you weren't expecting.

2. Encourage Design Thinking on Your Team.

It used to be that only the managers were involved in the design thinking process, which shouldn't be the case since all team members have different experiences and expertise. Also, making everyone involved in the product or process design, bring people together, and create inclusivity.

In the end, design thinking is about understanding the problem, asking questions, and creating solutions, therefore, anyone on the team should be encouraged to take an active role while giving them the design thinking training they need to perform following the 5 design thinking stages.

3. Encourage Rapid Failure

Design thinking is continuous. It's a process of rapid iteration taking lessons from the experiences to reach the best possible solution in a short time.
You need to take action and accept what's wrong, create the feedback loop and continue improving while making sure that employees aren't penalized for making mistakes during the process.

Testing and the feedback loop should be done periodically each time making improvements along the way. This way, you will have a much better product in a short time and your team will feel inspired seeing the progress.

A concise way to approach design thinking to implement OKRs into your organization using the synergy of your team is: " Empathize, Invent and Experiment".

4. Mind Mapping

Mind mapping is a graphical presentation of developing new ideas and building a tree-like visual architecture for seeing the big picture of ideation.

Mind Mapping was first popularized by Tony Buzan, the British author, and TV personality, in the 1970s, by his book: Modern Mind Mapping for Smarter Thinking.

The major advantage of mind mapping is that it makes creating and understanding new concepts extremely easy since the entire content is broken down into pieces and the content is visual and concise.

To use mind mapping for OKRs, the main thought in mind is your Objective, which breaks down into Key Results, Sub-key Results, and Initiatives. A thoroughly designed mind map of your Key Results is what makes your Objectives achievable.

It also gives you a bird's-eye view over your entire project gaining you a better insight while not leaving out anything important.

There are quite a number of mind mapping software, however, it may also be designed on a sheet of paper, if done, individually. The top 3 software you can use for mind mapping is Mindmeister, which is integrated into Google Drive, Lucidchart, and Miro. They all have free versions and different features that can serve as a great mind mapping tool to implement your Design Thinking process and OKRs.

How Companies 10x Their Performance via OKRs

Defining the Top Objectives

The ultimate goal is the North Star of the company that is designed for a long-term goal, which could extend to 10 to 20 years in the future.

A good example of an ultimate objective can be John F. Kennedy's top priority and "Moonshot Goal": "Before the decade is out, land a man on the moon and return him safely to earth." This clear and audacious goal brought all the country together to achieve the seemingly impossible and the first moon landing was achieved by Neil Armstrong and Buzz Aldrin on July 20, 1969, which was known to become "One Giant Leap for Mankind".

OKRs bring discipline in thinking for the future while building focused and concise communication throughout the company letting everyone know what really matters.

OKRs qualify the top priorities with the objectives and quantify the performance to reach those objectives with key results. Initiatives are the actions taken to fulfill the KRs.

As the "What" for the company is answered with the Objectives using one concise, immeasurable and challenging sentence, the idea of the ultimate objective needs to create the direction. The leadership needs to agree that the ultimate objectives are the top priorities and they need to commit completely to building an example for the rest of the company.

As the top objectives and key results are agreed upon, the rest of the company can build their department, group, and individual objectives independently while always bearing in mind the ultimate objective of the company as the end goal and how their objectives, as well as their key results, are aligned with the top objectives.

Each department, team, and individual need to have 3 to 5 objectives at most. Ambitious companies may think that they can achieve more objectives, but after 40 years of research and experience, the right number for objectives is 3 to 5.

The Hierarchy of OKRs

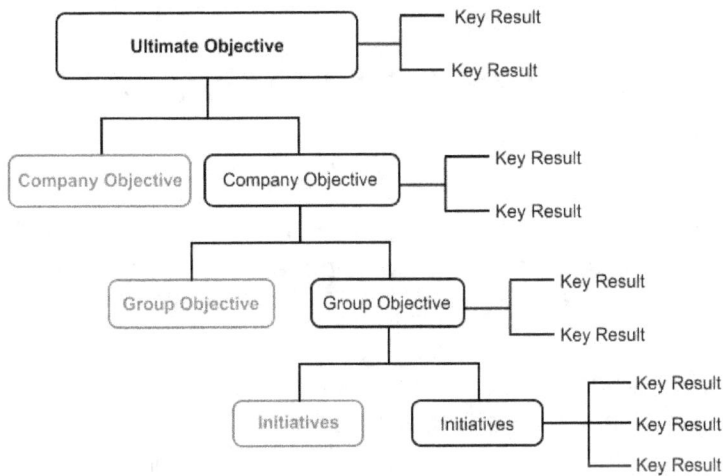

How Objectives, KRs and Initiatives Connect with Each Other

Setting Company OKRs

The ultimate objective is followed by 3-5 company objectives, which have a time span of 1 to 3 years. Company objectives set the direction for the entire organization.

To set the company OKRs, the leadership needs to ask the feedback of all the employees for the top priorities. Employees may use post-it, Google Documents, or even a whiteboard to share their concise feedback.

As all the employee insight is collected, the top 3 to 5 feedback can then become the company objectives.

Setting Team and Individual OKRs

The final part of the OKR goal-setting is for the team and individuals, which is built to help realize the long-term objectives of the company.

It is important to check and update OKRs regularly so that the company stays on track with regard to results while staying focused on realizing the company's long-term goals.

OKRs gain the organization a sense of purpose and accomplishment. It also gains the company the focus it needs by being able to say "No" to things. All company employees focus on 3-5 objectives at a time, therefore, they are able to say no to what's not their objective.

Key Characteristics of Objectives

Objectives are the top priorities that answer the question "What?", set the direction, and inspire with a concise sentence.

Aligned. As the ultimate objective is created, all other objectives should be built in the direction of the top objective aiming to realize it in the most productive and creative way making sure that all the company objectives are open within the company, checked regularly, and updated as needed to align with the ultimate objective.

Visionary. Objectives create the direction in which the company wants to go in the long term. Objectives create high-impact goals and an inspiring vision for the whole organization to follow and get motivated.

Time-bound. Objectives gain time discipline as well as directional discipline for the entire organization by creating challenging yet achievable deadlines. The ultimate objective may have a deadline of up to 25 years whereas company department objectives may have a shorter time span of 1-3 years. Teams and individuals may have deadlines of 3-12 months.

Checking the objectives monthly and building the feedback loop are also what make objectives effective and OKRs impactful in the long term.

Key Characteristics of Key Results

Key Results are the means to reach ambitious objectives that answer the question "How?", create the strategies again with a concise sentence.

Specific. Each objective having 3-5 KRs, Key Results are how objectives are going to be achieved quantifying the performance exactly so that the results are measurable exactly and objectively.

High Impact. Key Results need to be as audacious as the objectives themselves so that they create the impact and challenge needed to realize the objective - still being achievable.

Serving the Purpose. If the objective is creating user-generated content through social media, the KR needs to specify how many UGC to be created through which social media channels reach how many users while keeping the engagement rate at a certain high.

Key Characteristics of Initiatives

Initiatives are action-oriented and they describe exactly how the KRs will be achieved.

Specific. Initiatives are action-based and explain exactly how the Key Results will be achieved.

Quantitative. Initiatives are measurable the same as Key Results. Initiatives need to be perfectly clear and scheduled for the company to reach a certain number.

OKR CHECKLIST

General

- Set quarterly / annually
- Openly available for all the company
- Objectively measurable by quantification and grading
- Set at personal, team, department, and company levels
- Used as a feedback system. Not associated with compensation and not a performance evaluation weapon.
- Creates alignment by mutual agreement.
- Continue incomplete KRs only if they're still important and serving the objective.

Objectives

- Each objective is one concise, well-thought-out sentence.
- Inspiring and long-term top priority.
- Openly shared with the entire company.
- Feels a tad uncomfortable to reach, yet still achievable.
- Set quarterly and annually.

Key Results

- Measurable and specific
- Ambitious
- Serving the objective.
- Checked and updated regularly as needed.
- Created so that the success can be graded by any software or individual objectively
- 0.6 to 0.7 is the target
- Process matters more than the score
- Scoring reinforces commitment throughout the company.

Initiatives

- Measurable and specific to the extent that how you achieve the KRs is crystal clear.
- As ambitious as the objectives and KRs building their achievability.
- Should be checked and updated regularly so that feedback is provided to make any updates to reach the objective.

Timeline

- The leadership defines the upcoming year's OKRs at the end of Q4 and closes the annual OKRs.
- Departments, teams, and individuals define the OKRs of the upcoming year at the beginning of Q1.
- OKRs are supported and KRs are implemented by related departments through initiatives.
- Weekly OKR check-ins are made with a fast feedback loop and updates as needed.

- This OKR cycle is repeated annually.

How Grading Works

Key results need to be concise and measurable such as:
1. Growing the active weekly users by 30%
2. Reducing the bounce rate to 35%
3. Opening 12 new physical stores

The most important principles of OKR grading is as follows:

- KRs need to be ambitious and considerably challenging to achieve.
- Grading is made between 0 to 1 and if the team achieves 1.0 easily, that's not a well-designed OKR.
- Grading is done by a team or individuals.
- It's also done by specific software especially for larger companies, however, a good OKR can still be graded objectively manually.
- Grading is about feedback and reassessment rather than the judgment of performance.
- Scoring throughout the organization creates ease of awareness and visibility of what's going right and wrong.

How to Create a Sustainable OKR Environment

OKR is an innovation management system that needs to be deeply immersed into the culture starting from the top executive team becoming an example to the entire company openly sharing their progress and checking on the departments' OKRs.

It's vital to bear the below in mind to build the long-lasting OKR culture:
- Leadership should be committed.
- Goals need to be ambitious, yet achievable.
- The top objective needs to have the ultimate vision in mind inspiring the team.
- Teams and individuals need to have the autonomy to answer the question: "How".
- OKRs need to be checked regularly making sure the feedback loop is fast and productive.
- 60% of the objectives should originate from the bottom up.
- All must mutually agree without dictating.
- The incomplete KRs should only continue if they still serve the objective as aimed.

How to Become an OKR Expert

As in most disciplines, you can become an expert on OKR by following the guidelines and practice.

As an Individual
Actually, it's easier to start adapting OKR into your life as an individual since it's all dependent on you, and not on outside factors such as alignment with the other employees and sub-OKRs.

All you need to do is become dedicated, gaining self-discipline and sincerity towards your OKRs, and following what's described throughout this book.

Questions you need to answer for annual OKRs
- What's your top objective?
- What are the 3-5 objectives that you need to achieve the top objective?
- What are the 3-5 Key Results for each objective that you created?
- What are the 3-5 initiatives you need to take to realize the above KRs?

As you determine your long-term OKR, then, you need to execute and inspect flawlessly.

Inspecting once a week to check your process is key along with the feedback you need to give yourself monthly.

From the moment you write down your OKR, you will feel more motivated and inspired. You will see that you will achieve incredible goals that you can only dream of just like Google and many other companies did.

OKR is the productivity and performance framework that you can use for your private and business life building for greatness and creating 10x change.

It's also best that you involve your friends and family in building OKRs so that you gain discipline and insight with their feedback while helping them learn and apply OKR for their lives.

Individual OKR Examples

Business

Objective. Build a design agency with robust content marketing

Key Result 1. Launch a Youtube channel and have 1000 subscribers in 3 months.

Key Result 2. Create an Instagram account and launch 2 giveaway contests each month to build user-generated content.

Key Result 3. Work with 10 content creators on Youtube and Instagram with a budget of $10,000 for 3 months.

Initiatives. Post every two days in each platform and blog for the next 3 months, cross-promoting and automating content.

Family

Objective. Organize family adventure trips every 3 months.

Key Result 1. Book vacation rental and flights with a budget of $2,500, 2 months in advance.

Key Result 2. Organize your work so that you can take one week off, while increasing your sales commissions by $5,000 every 3 months.

Key Result 3. Build relevant new skills with your family every 3 months before the trip.

Initiative. Make a family union this week about a skill and adventure trip. Book a family course for the skill required.

Personal

Objective. Become an extraordinary communicator.

Key Result 1. Read the top 3 communication books: How to Win Friends and Influence People, I Hear You, and Unlimited Power in 3 months.

Key Result 2. Take courses of communication including the Tony Robbins course in 2 months.

Key Result 3. Listen 70% of the time in a dialog for the next month.

Initiative. Spend 2 hours a day reading the books.

How to Master OKR as a Company

OKR brings simplicity, openness, and alignment to any size company, which becomes a huge advantage for innovation and execution if the company embraces the powerful framework as it scales.

Leadership commitment. Top executives of the company should be fully committed to the OKR by:

- Creating ambitious, meaningful, and inspirational top objectives

- Making sure the departments are up to the task of applying the OKR system into their working environment.

- Opening their OKR and becoming an example by performing highly.

Consistency

OKRs take time and focus. As the leadership defines the annual OKRs, they need to consistently make sure that the rest of the company follows the OKR guidelines helping the top objective become a reality. One of the most essential parts of an OKR framework is that it gains focus and clarity. The maximum number of objectives should be no more than 5 and each one should be clear and concise.

Ambitious

One of the best benefits of the OKR system is its ability to create its own reality distortion field by reflecting what's seemingly impossible, likely possible.
As the company determines the "What" by defining the audacious top goal, employees create the answer for "How" while also benefiting from the open synergy of objectives and key results throughout the company.

Feedback Loop

To create rapid and productive progress, feedback should be provided by the related departments, teams, and individuals weekly or as soon as the key results are completed. This way, necessary updates can be made such as reshaping the execution without losing time and if needed, the OKR can be changed or even discontinued if it doesn't serve the objective.

Open Culture

All OKRs need to be made open at all times so that everyone in the company can check the progress made, see if they're aligned and give feedback as needed. Most of the time, if the company isn't open, employees become unaware of the top priorities and progress made.
Therefore, keeping the doors and communication open while assigning challenging, yet achievable goals creates the bond and the connected company that Google and many other companies created while having tens of thousands of companies, yet running like a startup taking initiatives to mainly realize the top objective.

Free Space

The traditional company structure is from top to bottom. This hierarchical build-up creates a lack of understanding and commitment from the top-down since all goals and actions are defined mainly by the exec team.

Instead, when the company is created from the bottom-up, then, as the top objective is defined by the leadership, the rest of the company creates its own objectives and key results to realize the top priority. This creates a much better understanding, more meaning, and responsibility along with creativity and inspiration for the entire company. Department and team managers check on the progress.

Ideally, 60%+ objectives are created from the bottom-up. This creates a sense of ownership and innovation at all levels of the company making people believe they can create change that matters since people face their own challenges at their work and they are the best people to know the solutions for those problems.

How to Implement CFR for Continuous Performance Management

According to John Doerr who made OKR grow into a global phenomenon starting from Google, CFRs complete the OKR system to create a "Continuous Performance Management".

CFR stands for Conversations, Feedback, and Recognition. CFRs provide the context for important discussions around the critical team and organizational objectives.

CFRs answer the question "Why?" behind the "What?".

CFRs give OKRs the voice they need so that the communication creates the highest value.

Conversations

A focused and open dialog between the manager and contributor is key to making sure the goals are aligned and the team is on the right to achieve the goals.

Be consistent. Weekly conversations are ideal, making your schedule consistent while building close relations with your peers.

Listen. We listen, we learn. As you listen to the progress and feedback, you can add higher value and you would also receive more respect from your employees because they will feel their voices are heard.

Empathize. Emotional intelligence is key to creating high-value conversations. Be open to new ideas and feedback. What matters is you achieving your goals together as a team. When people feel that ego is left out, real progress for the product is made.

Conversation Examples.
1. We aim to reach $5M sales per month in 3 months. I see that you are achieving your key results except for one. How do you plan to achieve the cross-promotion key result?

2. We are very close to reaching our battery cell cost reduction goal, thanks to your team's hard work. What are the next steps you're planning to take to reach the goal on time?

Feedback
It is vital to create bidirectional communication with respect to the progress made and the possible improvements that can be designed and executed.

How to Design a Great Feedback Loop
Frequent. When the feedback is frequent, it becomes a part of daily life, resulting in better communication and implementation. Make your feedback as just-in-time as possible making it a part of your personal and team culture.

Be specific. Top results and success can be achieved when your feedback is clear so that specific actions can be taken toward the goal. It's best to give feedback that's achievable.

Don't sugarcoat. When you try to be positive all the time, then, there may be misunderstandings. What matters is getting the best product done with a certain timeframe in mind. You need to give constructive feedback that's sincere.

Feedback Examples
1. "Jack, it seems you will be able to achieve all your Key Results on time and be in the green zone for Q2, however, we may not be able to achieve the quarterly objective. We may want to adjust your KRs."

2. "Audrey, you seem to need some help on your Key Result that involves content creation for social media engagement growth. I will make sure you and Allison have a meeting this week. You two can create the right strategy for sure."

Recognition

It's incredibly important to celebrate the success of deserving individuals by expressing appreciation. Recognition is possibly the easiest component of CFR to implement. 81% of employees say they feel more motivated to work harder when their managers show appreciation.

Recognize small wins. A simple thank you, a short email or a Slack message goes a long way to build lasting relationships and devotion.

Be timely and authentic. There's no better way to communicate and build relations with your peers other than showing appreciation by spending time writing a message for them making them feel special and appreciated for their hard work.

Encourage peer-to-peer recognition. For the company bonding and communication to thrive, it's important that all the companies feel like a team and when peer-to-peer recognition occurs, the real connection can take place.

Examples for Using Recognition with OKRs
1. "Natalie, you're an inspiration for your team, not only because you work so hard and achieve great results, but you also motivate everyone around you. On behalf of all the team, I want to thank you!"
2. "Hugo, you have made great progress in only a month. I really appreciate the extra hours and creativity you put into your work to achieve this quarter's goals. Thank you!"

The Best Free and Paid OKR Tools / Softwares

OKRs don't need very advanced building and tracking software especially when it's executed for an individual or a small company.

If you are just getting started, you may simply use free tools and when you scale, you can move onto the paid software that offer more advanced features.

Google Docs / Google Sheets

Google Docs / Sheets is the free, simple, and effective way to openly build your OKRs especially if you have a small team or you want to adopt OKR for your personal life.

John Doerr and his team of What Matters have made a free template for both Google Docs and Google Sheets. Simply open the Google Doc template here and Google Sheets template here.

To use:
- You need to be signed in to your Gmail account.
- Select "File" and "Make a Copy" from the drop-down to start filling in your own objectives and key results./

Koan

Koan.co
Unrestricted free version available.
Capterra review: 4.8/5
Koan offers an organizational alignment software platform that helps teams manage goals and status collaboratively. The Koan software was created to build strong teams with a focus on transparency, collaboration, feedback and empowerment. You can learn more here.
See how Koan works in this video.

Coda

Coda.io
Free version and template available.
Available on iOS and Android
Coda is a collaborative document solution that offers the flexibility of a document, the power of a spreadsheet, creating databases, and team collaboration using an intuitive user interface.

Coda and John Doerr have teamed up to offer a free introductory template for teams. You can open it using your Gmail account here.

Weekdone

Weekdone.com
Starts from $10/mo per person.
Capterra review: 4.5/5

Available on Android and iOS.
The objective of the Weekdone OKR software is to implement OKR best practices by keeping team OKRs in focus with weekly check-ins and weekly reports.
You are able to see how everyone's OKRs are progressing with weekly progress reports and live dashboards.
Weekdone also offers unlimited OKR coaching.
See how Weekdone works in this video.

Plai

Plai.team
Capterra review: 4.6/5
Desktop-based. $5/mo per active user.
Plai is the final software I recommend that aligns and focuses on teams with OKRs. It has tools to grow your team with regular feedback. Plai also works with what you use such as Slack, Google, or MS.
See how Weekdone works in this video.

OKRs vs Other Top Performance Systems

Even though OKR is the complete and most popular performance framework among the most innovative companies, it's useful to know about the other performance systems to be able to interpret the overall performance management ecosystem.

OKRs vs KPIs

OKR is a strategic framework, whereas KPIs are measurements that exist within a framework.

- KPI is generally a single data point whereas OKR refers to a strategic framework that tracks the achievement of a goal with specific metrics.
- KPIs are quantitative (and in rare cases, qualitative). They measure the progress and if the goals are reached successfully.
- KPIs are reviewed at the executive level. The key to KPIs is to measure the indicators with the most impact and value for the company.
- KPIs are measured against a target. Every KPI is measured aiming at a certain target within a time period to reach the goal.
- Every KPI needs to have a clearly defined data source so that there is no gray area.

KPI Examples

KPIs should be broken down by department if the company isn't very small.

Sales KPI Examples.
- Sales made through paid ads for the newly launched product.
- Average time needed for conversion

Customer KPI Examples

- Percentage of market share
- Average customer support resolution time

Marketing KPI Examples
- Number of blog posts published this month
- Number of user-generated posts

Apple KPIs
The biggest company in the world has the following KPIs
- Customer satisfaction
- Core competencies
- Employee commitment and alignment
- Market share
- Shareholder value

OKRs vs SMART

S.M.A.R.T. stands for specific, measurable, achievable, realistic, and timely.

In November 1981, George T. Doran wrote an article with the title: "There's a S.M.A.R.T. way to write management's goals and objectives," in the Management Review, which was the first time SMART goals were born. You can read the full article here.

OKRs connect key results to objectives and they're utilized to create strategies and tactics to achieve the objectives whereas SMART is a guideline to create objectives without having any connection to how those objectives are achieved.

It's best if an OKR is SMART by making the OKR specific and measurable, therefore, an ideal OKR would preferably contain the SMART system.

OKRs vs Balanced Scorecard

The balanced scorecard (BSC) is a management performance framework that has become popular in the last 25 years.

Even though both BSC and OKR share the same goal-setting and measures or key results to achieve those top priorities, they have major differences.

The major difference is that BSC is set for annual or longer-term goals whereas OKR is set mostly quarterly with a maximum period of 1-year managed and redefined by the management.
The other key difference is that when building a BSC, organizations construct objectives in 4 distinct, but related perspectives of performance, which are financial, internal processes, customer, and learning & growth. OKRs don't use these reference points and what matters is the achievement of the next quarter's goals.

Top Reads

Top OKR Sources

- Practice of Management - Peter Drucker (1954) - MBO
- High Output Management - Andrew Grove (1995) - OKR
- There's SMART Way (pdf) - George T. Doran (1981)
- The Balanced Scorecard (HBR) - Robert Kaplan (1992)
- Measure What Matters - John Doerr (2018)

OKR and Performance Related Top Books

- Lean In - Sheryl Sandberg (2013)
- Good to Great - Jim Collins (2001)
- Trillion Dollar Coach - Jonathan Rosenberg and Eric Schmidt (2019)
- Straight Talk for Startups - Randy Komisar (2018)
- How Google Works - Eric Schmidt & Jonathan Rosenberg (2017)
- In The Plex - Steven Levy (2011)
- Great by Choice - Jim Collins (2011)
- Work Rules - Laszlo Bock (2015)

Author's Books

Helium Network: The Best Crypto Mining Choice : Earn up to $10,000 per month passively anywhere in the world while building the People's Network of IoT and 5G:

Ebook

Paperback

The Best Video Learning Sources for OKR

- How Google Sets Goals - A Google Venture OKR Presentation
- Why The Secret to Success is Setting the Right Goals - John Doerr
- John Doerr on OKRs and Measuring What Matters
- How to Scale Your Business Using OKRs
- Ideas are Easy, Execution is Everything - John Doerr
- Measure What Matters - John Doerr
- Theory vs. Reality in OKR

References

- How Google Sets Goals with Objectives and Key Results
- OKR Case Studies
- Measure What Matters - John Doerr
- The Ultimate OKR Guide - Perdoo
- How VC John Doerr Sets Goals
- Objectives and Key Results - Everything You Need to Know
- How Spotify Brings Imagination to OKR Planning
- 10 Most Important Business Objectives
- Company-wide OKRs - What are Some Examples?
- Design Thinking - IDEO
- Design Thinking - What's Ideation?
- 5 Stages in the Design Thinking Process
- All About Mind Maps
- Measure What Matters - Mind Map
- Mindmeister Mind Map App
- Miro Mind Map App
- KPI vs OKRs - ClearPoint Strategy
- Apple KPIs
- OKRs vs Smart Goals
- OKRs vs Balanced Scorecard
- The 4 Secrets of OKRs that Actually Work

About the Author

Saygin Celen is a mechanical and industrial engineer who is passionate about design thinking and digital technologies. He has worked in the automotive and renewable energy industries as an engineer. His love of design urged him to create an architectural solutions company, design and kickstart his own sneaker brand successfully, and designing and consulting for machinery companies.

He is the co-founder and CEO of the digital creative agency, AwayNear and currently, he works with a top digital talent team to build digital development, business, and marketing solutions for startups around the world.

As a keen follower of the Google business, technology, and innovation, Saygin became highly interested in how small to large companies run and create disruptive innovation. As OKR was at the crossroads of innovation and management for any Google business and many top companies, he read and analyzed the books written by the leading OKR experts, learned from other video, and media sources and applied Objective and Key Results into his business and personal life seeing its extraordinary results that would otherwise be not possible.

Finally, he decided to share the knowledge, insight and experience he gained in time with the people who are open to innovating their business and personal lives.

www.ingramcontent.com/pod-product-compliance
Lightning Source LLC
Chambersburg PA
CBHW070455220526
45466CB00004B/1840